Christmas 1992

Dear Aunt Mary Kay and Uncle Bill,

    Here's what an Aussie Christmas is like for us. We'll try to beat the heat at the beach and blend in with all the Australians doing the same.

       Love,

          Colleen, Earl, Camden and Connor.

Christmas in
AUSTRALIA

Editor & Project Director: *Malcolm McGregor*

Associate Editor: *Jeanni Wright*

Designer: *Deborah Brash*

Text: *Rob Walls*

Office Christmas picnic, Palm Beach, N.S.W. GRAHAM MONRO

D URING the Christmas period of 1989, a group of 60 Australian photographers, both amateur and professional, geared up to record an event that in itself is not essentially unusual. In fact, it is an event that has been celebrated every year since the arrival of white settlers in this country.

This Christmas was unusual, in that never before in Australia had anyone attempted such a co-ordinated visual record of a national celebration. The photographers practised their skills from the outback to the cities; amongst their own families; on farms and in churches; in refuges for the poor and needy. They photographed the joy that Christmas brings to the young and the warmth that parents experience in making this event so special to their children. They photographed the unique aspects that make Christmas in Australia different from the event that is celebrated in the northern hemisphere.

In the two centuries since first settlement, Australia has become home to almost every nationality on earth. It has done so with an ease and grace that is an example to the rest of the world.

Christmas here has been altered and burnished by the customs of the new settlers. Separated from the mainstream of custom and in a climate that is the reverse of tradition, Christmas in the Antipodes has emerged as national holiday as much as religious event. Indeed this is the four week period in which the majority of Australians take their annual vacation. Its importance in the calendar of a young country without the trappings of a long and turbulent history, is in many ways more intense than it would be in an older nation.

From almost 15,000 images the following pictures have been culled. They provide a definitive record of how we Australians, old and new, celebrate Christmas.

Carols by Candlelight, Darlington, W.A. RICHARD WOLDENDORP

John Martin's/State Bank Pageant, Adelaide. Tony Lewis

Manly Beach in pre-Christmas heat, Sydney. GEOFF SWAN

Hutchinson Australia
an imprint of
Random Century Australia Pty Ltd
20 Alfred Street, Milsons Point NSW 2061

Sydney Melbourne London
Auckland Johannesburg
and agencies throughout the world

First published 1990

Conceived, designed and produced for the publishers
by J. M. McGregor Pty. Ltd., Queensland, Australia.

National Library of Australia
Cataloguing-in-Publication Data

Christmas in Australia.

ISBN 0 09 169810 3.

1. Christmas — Australia — Pictorial works. 2. Australia
— Social life and customs — Pictorial works.

394.2682820994022

Editor and Project Director: Malcolm McGregor
Associate Editor: Jeanni Wright
Designed by Deborah Brash/Brash Design
Text by Rob Walls
Typeset by Savage Type, Queensland
Printed by South China Printing Co., Hong Kong
Participating photographers used FUJICHROME film.

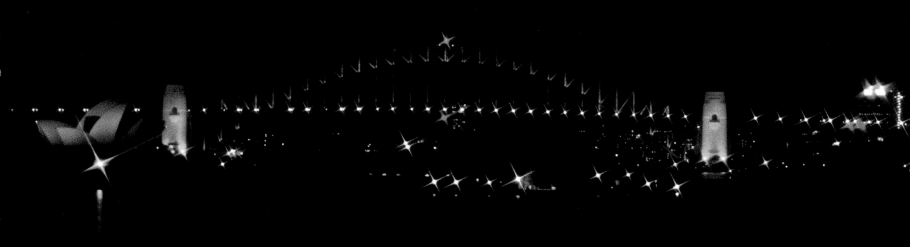

Sydney Harbour. MELISSA McCORD

Carols by Candlelight, Parramatta Stadium, N.S.W. TREVERN DAWES

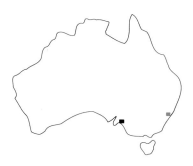

▪ Could it be that the Gerhard Berger team at the Adelaide
Grand Prix is the training ground for Santa aspirants?

BRIAN PLUSH

▪ A tidy of the whiskers before appearing at Sydney's Carols by
Candelight in the Domain. Santa Gavin Smith is one of the more
authentic and believable characters in the role and is much in
demand.

ROWAN FOTHERINGHAM

The 150 residents of White Cliffs in the N.S.W. outback are mostly miners and live underground. Michelle & Peter Hornby live in a 6 roomed home (with a granny flat) 6 metres below ground level with the temperature a constant 20–21°C year round, despite the outside temperatures of 40°C plus. When they need more space they simply dig it out.

The solar panels provide electricity for the local residents of one of the most arid and hot areas of the continent.

STUART OWEN FOX

■ The Wilcannia Catholic Community School is run by nuns from the Sisters of Missionaries of Charity. It caters at the levels of kindergarten to Grade 2 for the local Bakandji tribe. They hope to let the tribe run it themselves as several aboriginal aids are undertaking teacher training.

Timothy Bugmy dressed as Santa but all the children seemed to know who he was despite the thick cottonwool beard – it was 38°C that day.

The teachers and nuns organised a concert preceding the gift giving.

Luke Matysek

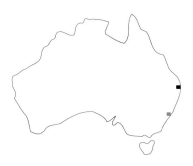

■ The Brisbane Mall has altered the nature of the city
dramatically. It now bustles with life and vibrancy. Christmas
crowds were continuously entertained from this stage and also
by numerous buskers.

JOHN LUKAC

■ Over 100,000 Sydneysiders attend the Esso Carols in the
Domain each year. The Salvation Army sell the candles, the
proceeds from which started 'Careline' in 1984, which in turn
has developed into the Youth & Drug Alcohol Counselling
Services.

ROWAN FOTHERINGHAM

■ Amazingly, at the last official ceremony for the year at Government House, Canberra, out of nowhere, hopped this kangaroo.

HEIDE SMITH

■ After the Midnight Eucharist, Christmas Eve, St. John's Anglican Church, Toorak. This service is quite a social occasion, attended by some of Melbourne's better known families and identities and is conducted by Archdeacon Philip Newman.

RENNIE ELLIS/*Scoopix*

■ Rev. Bruce Gray during the Pageant of the Nativity with Carols by Candlelight at the Anglican Christ Church, Keilor, Victoria. For the first time ever, the Anglican Churches of St. Martin's and Christ Church joined with the Keilor St. Stephen's Uniting Church in celebrating the birth of Christ.

JEFF CROW/*Impressions*

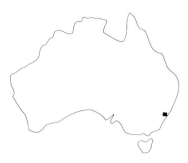

■ Typical of hundreds of Sydney suburban beer gardens, the Newport Arms is a popular place to drown a thirst, brown a body and generally to inspect the talent.

GRAEME GILLIES

■ Variety Club Christmas party for disadvantaged children.

RENNIE ELLIS/*Scoopix*

Suburban home, Cairns, Queensland. ROBERT GRAY

▪ This busker outside the David Jones' Elizabeth Street department store attracts attention — not only yuletide attention but also for the various causes his pavement pamphlets and placards proclaim.

ROB WALLS/*Rapport*

▪ Butcher Dennis Cassidy's Christmas actually begins in September, when he starts smoking hams in his smokehouse at Mullumbimby, N.S.W. He uses pine sawdust for the flavour. He works from the town's oldest butcher shop, built in 1927, where townspeople came to buy ice. After 17 years in the trade, his reputation for quality hams means he is exhausted by Christmas Day.

STUART OWEN FOX

▪ Preparing for Grace Bros Christmas parade, Sydney.

Trevern Dawes

■ The Campbelltown Concert Band ignores the downpour. This Grace Bros Christmas parade in Sydney included 15 floats, each supporting groups of performers and celebrities — a total of 1,200 persons. Police estimated crowds at up to 200,000.

TREVERN DAWES

▪ You would be forgiven for thinking the newspaper headline refers to the weather rather than the Berlin Wall.

TREVERN DAWES

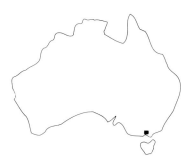

■ The window displays of the Myer Stores have become a 'must' for family viewing at Christmas. Each year a different theme is pursued — this year it was 'Alice in Wonderland'. What next?

ROB WALLS/*Rapport*

■ Gordon Ryan is the creator and designer of the characters which go to make up the Myer displays. His imagination and the industry of his staff are amply rewarded by the acclaim from wherever the stores are located.

JOHN KRUTOP/*Impressions*

■ The Victorian branch of the Variety Club of Australia, comprised principally of members of the acting and media professions, each year provides a wonderful party for disadvantaged children. Supported by dozens of local business houses, there is lots of laughter and entertainment and the children get to meet personalities they recognise from films and television — altogether a very big day in their lives.

GARY LEWIS

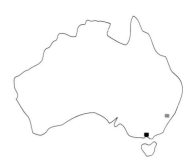

▪ A Japanese film crew from the 'Go Shoot Film Co', Nippon Television, recorded Santas in training at David Jones. Although David Jones have had Santas in their stores since 1907, their training school has been functioning only since 1985. They use about 26 Santas in their stores in N.S.W. with an age range of 18 to mid 70's. Prerequisites are a liking for children, understanding, friendliness and a sense of humour — some Santas have been heard to tell children that other Santas are merely helpers named Jack Claus or Bob Claus!

MATTHEW McKEE/*Rapport*

▪ After the Powell family Christmas dinner, Jamberoo, N.S.W.
BRUCE HART/*Rapport*

▪ It's thirsty work in the heat of Rockhampton, Queensland.
JOHN CASEY

Carols by 'Stars of the Australian Opera' — Queen Victoria Building, Sydney.
MATTHEW McKEE/*Rapport*

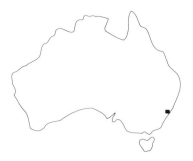

▪ Christmas Eve, Children's Hospital, Camperdown, Sydney.
JOHN PEEL

▪ Angels, Gemma Amos, Rebecca Lumley and Lauren Amos
at the Punchinello, Sydney, pre-school nativity play.
GEOFF SWAN

▪ With not a flake of snow to be seen, Santa had no need of his sleigh or reindeer and appeared on a boat at the start of the Fremantle to Auckland leg of the Whitbread Round the World Yacht Race, on Christmas Eve.

Sailed every 4 years since 1973, this year's event was the longest ever, covering 32,932 nautical miles through ice, storms and dead calm.

Twenty-three yachts representing 18 nations competed in this fifth Whitbread, starting and finishing in Southampton with 4 stops on the way.

ROBERT GARVEY

▪ Myer store's choral tree, Melbourne.
GARY LEWIS

▪ Prior to Christmas there are literally dozens of young buskers on Melbourne streets. With school on annual vacation for six weeks at least, it's an opportunity to display talent and also to raise some cash for presents and vacation activities.

GARY LEWIS

■ Pageant of the Nativity on the steps of Christ Church, Keilor, Melbourne — a celebration held in conjunction with the Uniting Church. Children attending as spectators were also invited to dress as angels or shepherds to add to the atmosphere.

JEFF CROW/*Impressions*

▪ David Rixon, with his daughter Sally, of Goonengerry, N.S.W., raises Embden and Toulouse geese for Christmas dinners.

An interesting sidelight is that he is also a kiwi fruit grower, and he has trained his geese to be 'weeder geese'; that is, they are trained to eat the weeds between the rows of kiwi fruit. As a bonus, they put a pat of organic fertilizer here and there at no extra cost. Rixon also has them on lawn patrol, which cuts down his mowing time.

According to Rixon, the first word Sally ever said was 'Geese'.

STUART OWEN FOX

■ Viggo Pedersen, his wife, daughter, friends, two family cats and two family dogs, all watch the annual preparation of the family Christmas feast — a Rixon goose.

Viggo, originally an immigrant from Bornholm, Denmark, builds craftsman homes. They live in Main Arm, N.S.W.

STUART OWEN FOX

▪ The season of peace and good will! Protest demonstration in Sydney prior to Christmas.

MATTHEW McKEE/*Rapport*

■ Duty doctors and nurses relaxing at Bundaberg Base Hospital, Queensland.

RAY PEEK

▪ Australian Ballet School performs 'The Nutcracker Suite' at the Victorian State Theatre, Melbourne.

Founded in 1964 by Dame Margaret Scott, this national school for dance shares facilities with the Australian Ballet Company and provides approximately 90% of its members. After extensive auditions, successful entrants embark on a 3 year course leading up to their diplomas.

GARY LEWIS

▪ David Anthony and Geraldine Parker have a studio at Byron
Bay — and here present some non-conformist views of Christmas!

Suzanna Clarke

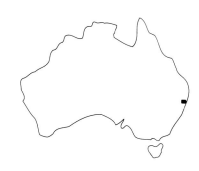

▪ Promoting a Christmas party for the nearby Station Hotel, Prahran, Melbourne.

RENNIE ELLIS/*Scoopix*

■ No matter how big you are they always put the rails in the wrong place!

Westfield, Chatswood, in Sydney's inner north, like hundreds of other shopping centres, displays traditional snow scenes despite summer temperatures in the 30's.

CRAIG KERSHAW

■ An early Christmas dinner for some of the less fortunate
Sydney residents.

ROWAN FOTHERINGHAM

■ Christmas reflection — one of the window displays of David
Jones' Elizabeth Street store, Sydney — promoted as "the most
beautiful store in the world".

RICHARD WOLDENDORP

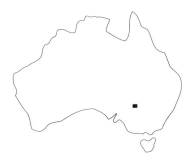

■ Santa arrives in the outback settlement of Silverton, 35 kilometres west of Broken Hill, with a camel train. The local kids turn out to see what's going on. "Ya can't fool us, those aren't reindeer," one of the kids said. "Nah, they're in disguise," Santa answered. The kids also wanted to know why Santa didn't have black boots — (no answer to that one).

Steven Cannard, 22, of Silverton is the Santa — it's the first time he ever played the part.

STUART OWEN FOX

A local tradition that has endured — one of several decorated homes on 'The Boulevard', Heidelberg, Melbourne. JEFF CROW/*Impressions*

■ Children from the Nauiyu Nambiyi community 150 kilometres south-west of Darwin, bathe in sweltering conditions of 43°C and 90 per cent relative humidity. They nevertheless must watch for crocodiles in the Daly River. One week after this photograph was taken a man was seized by the head in this locality and lived!

Whilst photographing here, the photographer dropped his Pentax 6 x 7 in the river and had to dive deep to retrieve it — a sobering thought. He said that had it occurred a week later the camera could have stayed there!

TERRY KNIGHT

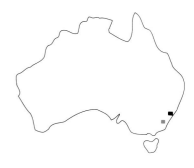

▪ You find the Sallys in all sorts of places — here they are providing foot-tapping, hand-clapping music at Paddy's Market reconstruction site in Sydney's inner city.

ROB WALLS/*Rapport*

▪ His Excellency the Governor General, Bill Hayden, addressing the Jewish community during Chanukah, Canberra, A.C.T.

GRAHAM GITTINS

▪ Each year the community of St. Ives, in Sydney's north, holds
carol singing and Santa arrives accompanied by the Kuringai
Bush Fire Brigade. In the mostly tinder-dry conditions of
summer, these largely volunteer brigades perform a vital and
often dangerous role.

GRAHAM MONRO

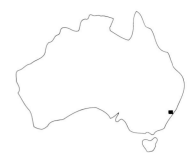

■ Russian Orthodox Church Mass, Cabramatta, Sydney, during the Epiphany, which celebrates the manifestation of Christ to the Wise Men of the East 12 days after Christmas.

BRUCE HART/*Rapport*

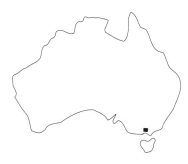

■ "Christmas at the Cathedral Church of Saint Paul, the Anglican Cathedral of Melbourne — very old and very beautiful. The state funeral of Harold Holt took place here, attended by the then President of the USA, Lyndon Johnson. A 'Life' photographer looking for a different shot removed a grille along the back wall almost at the ceiling. I went through the same steps. Three hours to remove the grille, chipping the mortar by hand to keep the noise down, as the Cathedral was open to the public. It was slow and difficult. Access was through the bell tower so I had to be in place one and a half hours before the start of the service. The service began and I had about 10 minutes to shoot. Three hours looking for the right position, 3 hours removing the grille and 1 hour replacing and remortaring the grille — all for 10 minutes' great fun."

JEFF CROW/*Impressions*

The Ashgrove Childcare Kindergarten and Preschool Centre, Brisbane. A delightful, well organised, heart warming place to visit. Their 'notes to parents' says . . . "We ask that children are dressed in play clothes suitable for our developmental experiences, which can be messy at times."

TONY BEE

■ **M**innamurra (an aboriginal word meaning 'place of many fish') is a sleepy village, 30 kilometres south of Wollongong. Nevertheless its school has 550 pupils and 19 staff catering to the populous surrounding area. On the final day of the school year, gifts are exchanged between teacher Gail Baker and her junior pupils.

ALAN POMERING

Christmas party at Wellington Square, for the less fortunate, provided by The Jesus People Inc. of Perth. RICHARD WOLDENDORP

■ The 'Tea and Sugar Train' which provisions the numerous isolated railway camps that dot the 2,000 kilometres of the Nullarbor Plain between Port Augusta and Kalgoorlie, is especially welcome at Christmas.

For 29 years, in sometimes stifling heat, Alf Harris has been the one and only Santa the camp children see. To them he's the dinkum one — no distractions of various department store varieties! Alf spends the year collecting and mending old toys to give the approximately 200 children something extra, added to the gifts of the Australian National.

David Dare Parker/*Auscape*

The annual 'Pier to Pub' 1.2 kilometre swim, from the old Fisherman's Pier to the Lorne Hotel, on Victoria's south coast. Approximately 2,000 participated in this fundraiser by the Lorne Surf Lifesaving Club.

RENNIE ELLIS/*Scoopix*

■ A chorister takes a break during proceedings at Christmas service St. Mark's Anglican Church, Darling Point, Sydney.

JOHN PEEL

■ The Shroot family have their private Chanukah celebration. Children get to eat pancakes called **latke** and play with skimming tops called **dreidles**.

The Jewish festival of Chanukah occurs in the period mid to late December. Like Christmas, it involves decorations, presents and rich foods. It celebrates the recapture of their Temple in Jerusalem in 165 BC by poorly armed but highly motivated Maccabees.

Whilst Christians talk of 'the twelve days of Christmas', Jews speak of 'the eight days of Chanukah'. The Menorah contains eight candles, one of which is lit each day until on the eighth day all are aglow. It is said that the candles denote concern for the young, for the poor, truth, liberty, justice, progress, humanity and beauty.

GRAHAM GITTINS

Carols by Candlelight, Melbourne. GARY LEWIS

■ Parish priest, Monsignor Walsh, conducted several masses on Christmas Eve at Our Lady of Victories Church, Camberwell, Melbourne. This beautiful church, built in 1918, contains 43 stained glass windows and possibly the best pipe organ in the Commonwealth.

To fund its construction, 65,000 'bricks' were sold at 10 shillings each and Pope Pius the Tenth purchased 50 pounds worth!

RENIE ELLIS/*Scoopix*

■ The Silverton Hotel, on the border of South Australia and New South Wales, is the only pub in town. Owned by Colin and Ines McLeod, the pub is famous as a location for numerous films (Mad Max, Razorback, etc.), commercials and for the eccentric people who visit — as well as horses. 'Misty' is an old horse that loves sticking her head in to see what's happening. Jake, the McLeod's 3-legged dog lives at the pub, and yes, he does like to water the odd tyre. At Christmas the McLeods erect a metallic Christmas tree outside.

STUART OWEN FOX

▪ The last Christmas mail being delivered to an outback Northern Territory station by Australia Post contractors, Air North. For the next three months many stations can be isolated by monsoon rains, with resultant flooding, so that mail delivery can then be hazardous and unpredictable.

The vast and rugged Northern Territory uses aircraft as a lifeline. Air North International is the largest commuter airline in the Northern Territory, operating over 25 aircraft. Scheduled flights service over 125 cattle stations and 20 remote settlements each week.

TERRY KNIGHT

▪ Northern Territory Aerial Medical Service staff, Sister Barbara Stott and Captain Bruce Percy transport patient Chris Day back to his home in the outback. The service is operated by the Northern Territory Department of Health and Community Services and over 12,000 patients are cared for each year. Free routine clinics and air ambulance services are provided by the government to cattle stations, mines and remote settlements. Similar services are operated in some other states by the Royal Flying Doctor Service.

TERRY KNIGHT

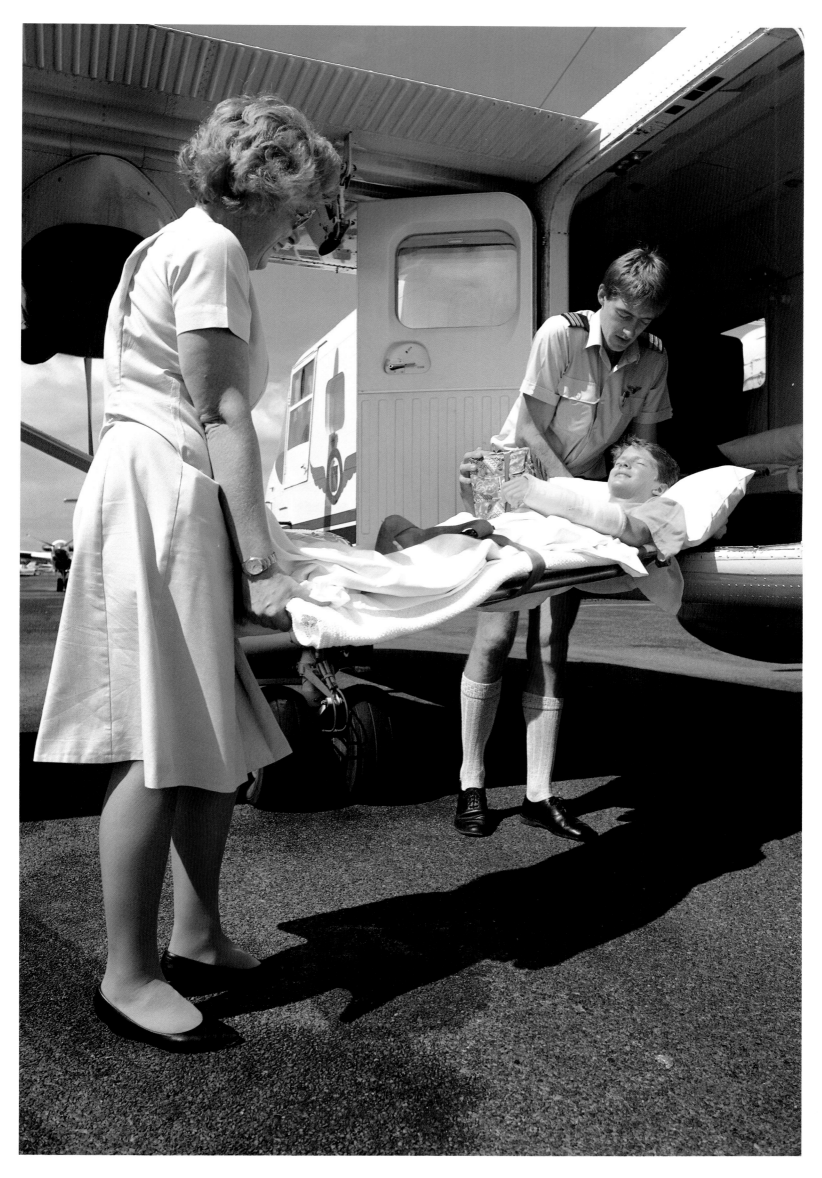

Christmas busking competition winners, the Kronk family, Toowoomba, Queensland. GRAHAM BURSTOW

■ Cricket fans at Melbourne Cricket Ground. A favourite form of relaxation over the Christmas holiday period.

RENNIE ELLIS/*Scoopix*

■ The accidental conjunction of a tourist promotion for
Papua New Guinea and an in-store santa provided a rather
bizzare scenario.

ROBERT GRAY

The Ivanhoe Grammar Memorial Junior School Choir.
TONY FEDER/*Impressions*

▪ With 10 days to go till Christmas, the International Mail Centre in Sydney was handling 800,000 inward letters a day and despatching 500,000.

Bob Napier is the champion manual sorter, reputed to sort 66 letters a minute. He has been on the job for 26 years.

In addition to sorting manually, a coding scanner handles 30,000 letters an hour and 50 temporary staff are added to help with the extra work load.

GRAIG GOLDING/*Sydney Morning Herald*

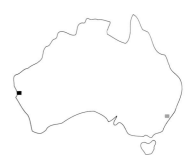

▪ The freedom of Christmas vacation at Shark Bay, 850 kilometres north of Perth.

DAVID DARE PARKER/*Auscape*

Quicksilver Diving Services, Port Douglas, Queensland.
CAROLYN WILLIAMS

■ Even angels get a little tired and not a little fed up having to carry heavy stars.

Carols by Candlelight and Nativity Pageant, Christ Church, Keilor, Victoria.

Jeff Crow/*Impressions*

■ Outside Brisbane City Hall. GRAHAM BURSTOW

Children's Youth Orchestra — Sydney. ROWAN FOTHERINGHAM

Blind Institute Carols — Perth, W.A. ROBERT GARVEY

'Camel Man' — Alice Springs, N.T. STUART OWEN FOX

Hard earned cash — Kalgoorlie, W.A. DAVID DARE PARKER/*Auscape*

Train Examiner — Cook, S.A.   DAVID DARE PARKER/*Auscape*

▪ Every year since 1922, volunteers have gathered at the Smith Family's head office to pack hampers for the needy, the lonely, the elderly, the battlers. Various business houses assist, using the gesture as part of their contribution to the Christmas spirit.

Over 7,000 hampers are delivered the week before Christmas in the Sydney area.

TREVERN DAWES

Christmas Eve, Greasy Joe's Cafe, Melbourne.
RENNIE ELLIS/*Scoopix*

• Christmas party at The Rocks, Sydney. One of the earliest settled areas in Sydney, originally containing a gaol built by convicts sent out to N.S.W. from Great Britain, The Rocks has been lovingly and faithfully restored and is now one of the most popular tourist attractions in Sydney. Most of the buildings are sandstone, as is the old Wool Store in the background.

TREVERN DAWES

▪ Too late to come to the aid of the party! Vanessa Van Keuk organised a Christmas celebration for the local kids in her Huonbrook, N.S.W., complex. She didn't plan for the mayhem. After this shot was taken a lamb wandered in and helped clean up the mess.

SUZANNA CLARKE

The Christmas atmosphere at Grace Bros.,
Chatswood store, Sydney. GRAEME GILLIES

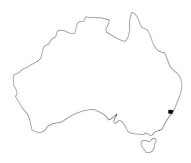

■ Twelve-year-old Ambre Lyn of Moss Vale taking advantage of her school vacation in Pitt Street, Sydney. She has passed her high level exams and now wants to buy a Steinway Grand!

MATTHEW McKEE/*Rapport*

A different form of busking. Here a pavement artist works with homemade pastel crayons. Some of the artists incur the wrath of civic authorities, although this man, by Hyde Park in Sydney, creates tremendous interest and admiration.

ROWAN FOTHERINGHAM

Snow White and the Seven Dwarfs — Melbourne. GARY LEWIS

▪ Four generations gathered together for the last Christmas of the '80s. From an eight month old baby girl to her 83 year old grandmother, they flew, they drove, they came by train — but they came, some of them travelling over 1,000 kilometres to be with the family on Graeme and Helena Stuart's property at Goonengerry, a tiny village in the scenic hinterland of Byron Bay.

STUART OWEN FOX

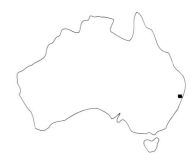

▪ The mid-week Dog Training Club in Sydney puts on a party,
not for the members, but for the dogs. Through shopping centre
demonstrations and appeals, the club this year presented $3,000
to the Guide Dogs Association — combined dog clubs presented
a total of $25,000!

After the presentation, each of the dogs — and there are nearly
200 at any given time — is called by name to receive its
Christmas present from beneath the tree.

DELAMERE USHER

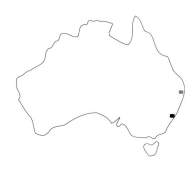

▪ Coolangatta, Gold Coast, Queensland.
GRAHAM BURSTOW

▪ Queensland Forestry Department tree cutters Gordon Hutchinson, Brian Kunst, Murray Bryce, Ken Matthews, Michael Burrow and Steven Wenbt have spent several weeks cutting and loading out yuletide pines at Beerburrum.

Seeds are grown in the nursery and planted onto disused fire breaks, spaced 3 metres apart. Planting about 15,000 a year they are grown for 3 years, then sold to service clubs such as Apex and Lions, to be used as fund raisers.

TONY BEE

**Detergent-created 'snow' provided by Kiama Fire Brigade —
Minnamurra, N.S.W.** Alan Pomering

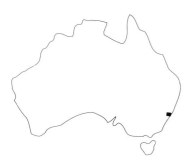

• In Toowoomba, Queensland, the local motor cycle club organised a procession to transport their gifts to charitable organisations, showing themselves as bikers not 'bikies'. As one Harley rider notes "when I see thousands of bikes and bikers lining the streets with toys and banners I see brotherhood at its best. To ride with pride, to give when most themselves are in need — that is brotherhood."

GRAHAM BURSTOW

■ More than 1,000 riders left Sydney's Rosehill Racecourse for the State Sport Centre at Homebush, preceded by Santa with a Sally in sidecar, to donate toys to the Salvation Army. This is the ninth year the N.S.W. Motorcycle Riders Association has staged the event called 'Help a Child to Smile this Christmas'.

CRAIG KERSHAW

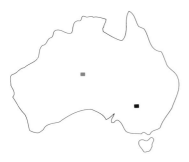

▪ Too young to drink it, but old enough to deliver it. Brendan Behsman and Leigh Mitchell unloading the Christmas supply at Wilcannia, 200 kilometres east of Broken Hill on the Darling River.

Lukas Matysek

▪ This old tucker bus is probably Australia's remotest and only mobile roadhouse. Situated on the banks of what is reputed to be the oldest river bed in the world, the Finke, the tucker stop is located about half way between Alice Springs and the Northern Territory border.

Bush ingenuity takes over when Christmas comes round. A Christmas tree consisting of a Desert Oak branch adorns the counter and the menu takes on a distinct bush Christmas flavour.

The bus is owned and operated by the Bliss family, who are rabbit shooters on nearby Henbury Station.

STEVE STRIKE

■ This F/A-18 Hornet of the RAAF 75th Squadron at Tindall Air Base, N.T. was given time off at Christmas.

WAYNE MILES

■ But prior to Christmas, 77th Squadron were busy on a mission out of Williamtown base, north of Newcastle. Squadron Leader Nick Anderson is on exchange from the RAF to the RAAF for a two and a half year stint.

GRAHAM MONRO

. . . and so to bed. Christmas Eve, Sydney. CRAIG KERSHAW

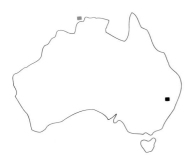

▪ The Tiwi Aboriginals have embraced Christianity into their culture and they make a point of celebrating Christmas. Richard Mungatopi is decorating his face for the church services on Melville Island, north of Darwin.

HEIDE SMITH

■ Amidst the hype of Christmas, 'Donkey Bob' travels around the New England area of New South Wales with his three 'symbols of Christmas' and his dog. His donkeys carry his worldly possessions and he camps under a tent-fly by the roadside. He is not a vagrant, but simply prefers to live this way. An educated and well read man, he dispenses some homespun philosophy on the way.

HAROLD KONZ

Esso's Carols in the Domain, Sydney. ROWAN FOTHERINGHAM

▪ An horrific road smash on the New South Wales north coast, just before Christmas, spread a pall over the whole country.

MATTHEW McKEE/*Rapport*

Australian Ballet School 'Nutcracker Suite' — Melbourne. GARY LEWIS

■ The Bushfire Brigade of Oak Flats raising funds at Lake
Illawarra, 10 kilometres south of Wollongong, N.S.W.

ALAN POMERING

Giles Weather Station is Australia's remotest meteorological recording base. It is manned by 6 personnel, 4 of whom volunteer for the location and stay for a period of 6 months.

The Station sits at the foot of the Rawlinson Ranges on the fringe of the Gibson Desert in Western Australia. Geographically, it is approximately half-way between Alice Springs, N.T. and Kalgoorlie, W.A. Its average yearly rainfall is 240 mm and the temperature at Christmas time is in the high thirties. The remoteness of the Station usually means spending Christmas alone — however for Christmas 1989 the Sheraton Resort at Ayers Rock, 2 hours' flying time away, decided the weathermen and their only female (the cook) deserved a full Christmas feast. So they flew in the works — the chef, turkey, ham, champagne — and even Santa himself made a brief appearance. A great party was had by all in a part of Australia's last frontier.

STEVE STRIKE

A toast on Christmas Day at Mawson Station, the earliest
established of Australia's Antarctic Outposts.

Jonathan Chester/*Extreme Images*

▪ The new Parliament Building in the nation's capital was deserted on Christmas Day, except for the luckless security guards. Canberra, A.C.T.

HEIDE SMITH

■ The long awaited rainfall, Christmas night — Mellaluca Station, N.T.
WAYNE MILES

■ "Let me guess! It's an elephant . . . a bulldozer?"
Joanne Ansel, Mellaluca Station.
WAYNE MILES

▪ Christmas Day street party at the Wayside Chapel, King's
Cross, Sydney, domain of nationally famous Rev. Ted Noffs. For
many years this chapel has assisted the downtrodden, drug
addicts, prostitutes, abandoned wives and children, and anybody
enduring hard times. This man and his organisation represent all
that is finest about practical Christianity.

GRAHAM MONRO

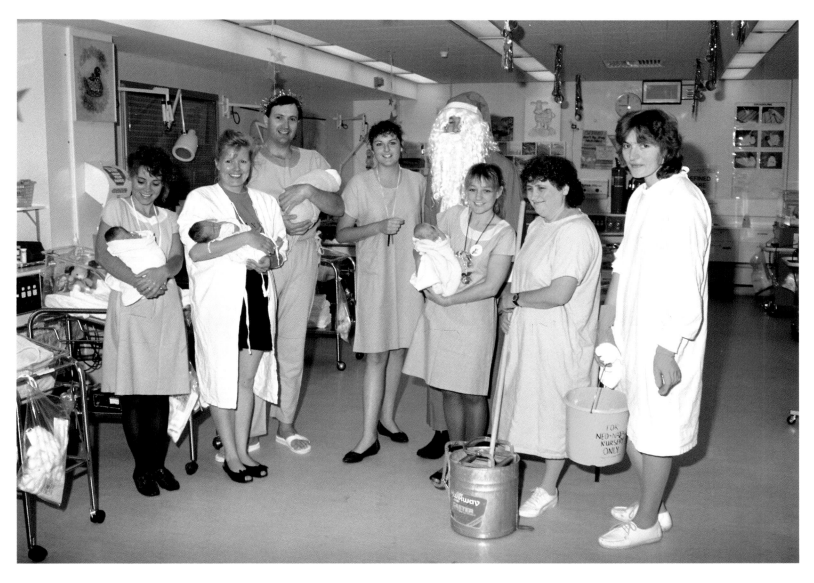

▪ The most precious gift of all. New lives on Christmas morning under the care of the ward staff at Royal Children's Hospital, Canberra, A.C.T.

GRAHAM GITTINS

■ Gift giving, early morning, at Mellaluca Station, 150 kilometres east of Darwin on Point Stuart.

Later in the day comes an enormous dinner for family and staff.

WAYNE MILES

▪ Father Wrona and Father Ted celebrating Polish Mass at St. Gregory's, Queanbeyan, N.S.W. Canberra has a sizeable settlement of Polish immigrants, many having worked on the Snowy scheme after the war.

GRAHAM GITTINS

▪ The Newcastle N.S.W. pub crawl starts at the Mary Ellen Hotel, Merewether, and moves towards Newcastle via the suburbs. The custom is for all Santas and helpers to pass out sweets and treats to kids they encounter en route between pubs.

Held on the Friday before Christmas, there were 260 starters this year.

'Carols are to be sung before leaving each venue.'

Peter Stoop

▪ A cuddly teddy is bound to receive a big bear hug anywhere in the world. Six-year-old Suzanne Cuerden of Perth, Western Australia, fell in love with hers the moment the wrapping paper was torn off.

ROBERT GARVEY

▪ Katherine and Christopher Broadway received their Christmas gifts in the home of their paternal grandparents at Eaglemont, Victoria.

JEFF CROW/*Impressions*

Christmas party of Melbourne's fashion industry at Cafe Cliquot, Carlton. RENNIE ELLIS/*Scoopix*

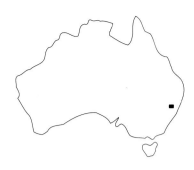

■ The village of Upper Horton, New South Wales, celebrates year's end with a two day rodeo. The dust, heat and flies do not dampen the action or the enthusiasm of the riders.

Harold Konz

■ "Now, have I got this right?"
Caroline Stewart helps out at the Longyard Hotel, Christmas Eve dinner — Tamworth, N.S.W. This hotel is a centrepiece of the Country & Western festivities held in Tamworth each January. It includes a tourist complex of brewery, ice cream parlour and golf course along with the pub, and in its front yard, facing the passing traffic of the New England Highway, is a giant, model golden guitar.

Alan Pomering

■ Christmas vacations at Mooloolaba Beach,
Sunshine Coast, Queensland.

John Peel

World's remotest course — Giles, W.A. STEVE STRIKE

Bronwyn Sellers — Launceston, Tasmania. MARK TRIPP

Cricket Test — Melbourne. TONY FEDER/*Impressions*

■ Some prefer solitude on their vacation. An early morning campfire of a lone bushwalker, 50 kilometres west of Twin Falls, Kakadu National Park, N.T. At 5 am the temperature was already 38°C.

TERRY KNIGHT

■ Ambrose John, originally from Mount Catt in Arnhem Land, is employed by Mellaluca Station owner Rod Ansel, as a buffalo catcher. Like the rest of the staff he spent Christmas Day at the station. Wayne Miles found him pursuing his craft activities after dinner.

WAYNE MILES

■ For these Tiwi Aboriginal women on Bathurst Island, Christmas dinner is a wallaby. It was, in fact, killed by a dingo but the women talked him out of it.

HEIDE SMITH

• Burmese identical twins, Kathy Song and Tammy Graham in Sydney celebrating their twenty-second birthday, which was on Christmas Day.

Jean-Paul Ferrero/*Auscape*

■ Celebrating their first birthday in Brisbane, Jean Mary and Zowie Alma Moselen were born 10 minutes apart on Christmas Day.

TONY BEE

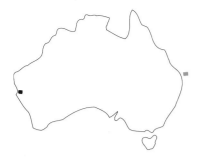

▪ Lady Musgrave Island is situated about 70 kilometres east of
Bundaberg in Queensland. It is the southern-most tip of the
Great Barrier Reef. One of the best ways to view the coral and
vast array of tropical fish is to snorkel in the warm, calm waters.

TONY FEDER/*Impressions*

■ David Parker spent part of his Christmas vacation at Shark Bay, 850 kilometres north of Perth. Like the tens of thousands of tourists who visit every year, he was captivated by the dolphins which swim into Monkey Mia to be fed and touched and to commune with humans. So familiar have they become that they have been given individual names — this is Nicky.

Completely free to cavort off into the Indian Ocean, they have chosen to remain. Nevertheless the sheer escalation of crowd numbers has caused doubt to be cast as to how long this extraordinary communication can continue.

Undoubtedly the dolphins themselves will decide the outcome.

DAVID DARE PARKER/*Auscape*

▪ Newcastle, N.S.W. A devastating earthquake occurred late morning on 28th December 1989, causing hundreds of millions of dollars in property damage. More tragically, for the first time in Australia's recorded history, the 'quake caused loss of life. Most of the 12 fatalities occurred in the Workers Club. Exhausted rescuers worked the clock around for days afterwards.

When a 'Jazz in the Domain' concert was held to raise funds for victims, as always the Salvation Army was there with assistance.

Graham Monro

■ During the holiday season, numerous surf carnivals are being held — ironman, surfing, life saving, board riding, etc. Despite its other problems, Sydney's Bondi Beach is still a mecca.

And what is a carnival without the obligatory Bathing Beauty contest?

MIKE LANGFORD

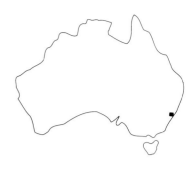

Christmas is a good time for older Tiwis to tell stories of the Dreamtime to the young. HEIDE SMITH

Participating Photographers

1 Robert Banks	33 John Lukac
2 Tony Bee	34 Melissa McCord
3 Graham Burstow	35 Steve McDowell
4 David Burton	36 Matthew McKee
5 John Casey	37 Luke Matysek
6 Jonathan Chester	38 Wayne Miles
7 Suzanna Clarke	39 Graham Monro
8 Trevor Creighton	40 Margaret Olah
9 Jeff Crow	41 Robin Osborne
10 Trevern Dawes	42 David Dare Parker
11 Rennie Ellis	43 Ray Peek
12 Tony Feder	44 John Peel
13 Jean-Paul Ferrero	45 Brian Plush
14 Rowan Fotheringham	46 Alan Pomering
15 Stuart Owen Fox	47 Peter Robinson
16 Robert Garvey	48 Lyn Roseby
17 Graeme Gillies	49 Wendy Saba
18 Graham Gittins	50 David Simmonds
19 Craig Golding	51 Michael Simmons
20 Stephen Gosch	52 Heide Smith
21 Robert Gray	53 Peter Stoop
22 Bruce Hart	54 Steve Strike
23 Michael Jefferies	55 Benjamin Stypel
24 Craig Kershaw	56 Geoff Swan
25 Max Klodinsky	57 Richard Thwaites
26 Terry Knight	58 Mark Tripp
27 Harold Konz	59 Delamere Usher
28 John Krutop	60 Anton Watts
29 Mike Langford	61 Rob Walls
30 Gary Lewis	62 Geoff Wharton
31 Tony Lewis	63 Carolyn Williams
32 Elia Loccisano	64 Richard Woldendorp

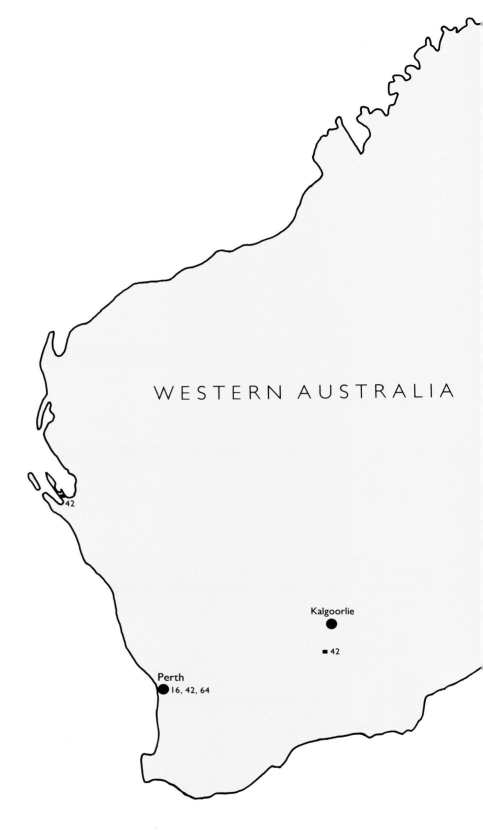

WESTERN AUSTRALIA

Kalgoorlie

■ 42

Perth
16, 42, 64

NORTHERN
TERRITORY

QUEENSLAND

SOUTH AUSTRALIA

NEW SOUTH WALES

VICTORIA

TASMANIA

52
Darwin ●
26, 38

■ 38
26, 38 ■

■ 26

Alice Springs
● 54, 64

■ 63
Cairns ●
21

Rockhampton
● 5

43 ■

■ 34

Brisbane
2, 3, 33
■ 3, 35
7, 15, 41 ■
27, 46 ■

42 ■

Broken Hill ●
15, 37

Newcastle ●
39, 53

Sydney
●
46 ■

4, 8, 10, 13, 14,
17, 19, 20, 22, 23,
24, 29, 32, 36, 39,
40, 44, 47, 48, 49,
51, 56, 59, 61, 64

Adelaide ●
31, 45

Canberra
● 18, 52

Melbourne ●
11, 50 ■

1, 9, 11, 12,
25, 28, 30, 55,
57, 60, 61

11, 37 ■

■ 58

Hobart ●
11, 62

12.01 am on 1st January 1990 — Sydney Harbour. GRAHAM MONRO